Counting the Black Angels

Counting the Black Angels

Poems by
Len Roberts

University of Illinois Press ◆ Urbana and Chicago

For my family

Publication of this book was supported in part by a grant from the National Endowment for the Arts

This book is printed on acid-free paper.

Library of Congress Cataloging-in-Publication Data
Roberts, Len, 1947–
Counting the black angels : poems / by Len Roberts.
p. cm.
ISBN 0-252-06381-3 (pbk. : alk. paper)
I. Title.
PS3568.02389C68 1994
811'.54—dc20   93-30476
                                                      CIP

Acknowledgments

My thanks to the editors of the following journals in which some of these poems, or versions of these poems, first appeared:

American Poetry Review: "He's Alone" and "The Way of the Cross"

Antioch Review: "Near the Paulite Church"

Boston Review: "Learning Animals and Insects in Third Grade"

Boulevard: "We Sat, So Patient" and "Joey McGraw's Desk, 1960"

Chelsea: "Walnuts" and "In the Field"

Chicago Review: "The Sparrow and *the Winter's Nest of Snow*"

Gettysburg Review: "Talking with God"

Hudson Review: "Second-Grade Angel," "Counting the Black Angels," and "On Hearing That We Were All Boundless, Unimaginable Energy"

Ohio Review: "My Mother's Guardian Angel"

New England Review: "What Sins, Now"

North Dakota Quarterly: "Holding Out the Hands"

Now This: "Clear January, zero degrees, my last"

Partisan Review: "Gift Shop in Pécs, Hungary"

Poetry East: "My son insisted"

Ploughshares: "Looking Up"

Poetry Northwest: "Learning the Stars" and "November Riffs, Wassergass"

Prairie Schooner: "After the Second Operation"

Quarterly West: "This and That"

Shenandoah: "The Coin Trick" and "When the angel
  finally came down"
Southern Poetry Review: "Reconsidering the Command-
  ments"
Virginia Quarterly Review: "Love on Lonesome Road"
West Branch: "Shrinking as they rise, the"
"Emma" appeared in the anthology *Catholic Girls and
  Boys,* published by Penguin/New American Library,
  1994.
"Gift Shop in Pécs, Hungary," appeared in *Pushcart Prize
  XVII: Best of the Small Presses, 1991.*
"Looking Up" appeared in a limited edition chapbook,
  Learning about the Heart, published by Silverfish Review,
  1992.
"The Way of the Cross" received first prize in the Wild-
  wood Poetry Contest, 1993.
"We Sat, So Patient" appeared in *Best American Poetry,
  1992.*

I am grateful to Yaddo and the John Simon Guggenheim
Memorial Foundation for residential and financial grants
that helped me to complete this book of poems. My
special thanks, too, to my wife, Nancy, for her patience
and encouragement, and to Hayden Carruth, Ken Fifer,
Philip Levine, and Gerald Stern for their continual
friendship, good advice, and support.

Contents

Part 1

We Sat, So Patient   3

This Spring   5

This and That   7

Trying to Tell My Mother about Her
   Guardian Angel   9

Second-Grade Angel   11

Holding Out the Hands   13

Near the Paulite Church   15

Joey McGraw's Desk, 1960   17

The Sparrow and *the Winter's Nest of Snow*   20

When the angel finally came down   22

My wife wants me to cut   24

Three Stars   26

Waiting for the voice or touch of God,   28

Splitting Wood with Milton and the Devils, Wassergass   30

Part 2

Counting the Black Angels   35

Walnuts   38

Gift Shop in Pécs, Hungary   40

Learning Animals and Insects in Third Grade   42

The Cowboy   44

Lee's Chinese Laundry   46

After the Second Operation   48

My Father's Fence   50

Shrinking as they rise, the   52

Emma in the Class on Reproduction   54

Talking with God   57

Bringing Ziggy His Homework after the Accident   60

Clear January, zero degrees, my last   62

Her Garden   64

The Coin Trick   66

The Way of the Cross   68

My son insisted   70

Learning Natural Instincts   72

Part 3

Looking Up,   77

It's All Right, It's OK   79

Killing Jesus   81

Love on Lonesome Drive Road   84

Pathways   86

Learning the Stars   94

He's Alone   96

The Tools   98

Reconsidering the Commandments   100

Rolling the World in St. Bernard's   102

In the Field   104

November Riffs   106

What Sins, Now   108

On Hearing That We Were All Boundless, Unimaginable
    Energy   110

Ready in Wassergass   112

Part 1

We Sat, So Patient

We sat, so patient, in that third
   grade
class, learning the numbers of days,
   weeks, months,
repeating the numbers as they flashed
   in the air, forming
the curved 3, the angular 4, the easy 1,
counting the raindrops that wriggled down
   the gray window,
counting the hearts and cars on our desks,
   our crayons,
Ann Harding and Richie Freeman making 2,
10 on each side for the spelling bee,
   counting silent
seconds when Sister Thomas said 5
   of us
would not reach 20, showed the chart
where children dropped off into 0,
   the blue zone of no return
that Jimmy Legasse whispered, making us laugh.
Looking around, I thought Al Aldon, Jackie Schuster,
   Margaret Blake
who already coughed blood on her gold glasses
   when she spoke,
the thin girl just come over from Germany,

and Ray Martineau who had no lunch, the
    zigzagged
white lines of lice forming mazes on his
    crewcut head. And
the good Sister herself, number 6, at least
    40 years older than us,
her rosary beads clicking as she walked
down the aisle like the Angel of Death,
    black
wings spread, brushing our faces, our arms,
    wafting blackness
into our eyes, our lungs, our hearts,
reminding us that God was watching and could tell
    who knew 9 times 9, 144 divided by 12,
telling us it was God's will that we die,
Jimmy Gleason pulling up his white sock
on a leg he would not have 10 years later,
Barbara McGill raising her hand with another
    correct answer,
the same hand so whitish-blue as she lay
    in her eighth-grade coffin,
Jimmy Amyot and Donald Wilcox quietly passing
    drawings of naked women
back and forth, the car they would die in
    revving
unheard in that classroom where we yelled
    out 360, 225, 32, 0, 10,
 waiting for the split-second flash of red,
    yellow, and blue cards
beneath the slow, steadily clicking clock.

This Spring

I've cut them all
  down,
white and pink daisies, bluebells,
  thistles
and daffodils, not like before
  when
I let them go, mowed around,
  gathered
them up for the cracked, empty
  blue
vase set on the round oak table.
  This
      Spring their weed-whacked
  heads
float in the pond, on the grass,
  across
the upper fields randomly, blues
  and
yellows and whites and golds—
There's no one about who's going to
  pick them up.
I'm down here sharpening the blades,
  wrapping more
orange string in the whacker's black
  head,

I'm whetting the scythe, too, for the
   easy sweeps
around the pond's edge, I'm turning
   into
a knife here in this brisk May wind,
   not afraid
to think of a hand getting in the way,
   snicking it
off, a foot, a leg, glad I've told
   my wife
to burn me when I die, to throw
away the ashes and bits of bone.

This and That

Now the snow falls and I walk up
    St. Bernard's steps,
determined to tell the good Father
    all of my sins,
the ones I'd held back since summer,
    too, and the ones
I'd thought, ordering them from best
    to worst,
peering at Lorraine undress at the
    start,
lying with Lorraine, naked, in the
    grass
behind Desormau's Packing Plant
    last, not
sure if I should mention how her hand
    stroked me
until I was dizzy and the sky reeled,
    not sure
if I had to tell how her sex smelled,
how I walked around for days lifting
    her on my fingers,
carrying her through geometry class
    and basketball
practice the way I held the holy chalice
those Sunday mornings I served high mass.
    Father, I said

to myself, I've done this and that, but
    then the snow
began to fall harder, large, wet flakes
    straight
down, feeling them on my wave of hair,
    my turned-up collar,
feeling them wash my face when I looked
    up
to see the gray sky ringing with bells
until lovely Lorraine drove by in her
    white Oldsmobile,
window down, waving, putting her signal
    light on
as she slowed by the yellow curb and I
    decided
to save my soul the following Saturday,
    wondering
how thick and slick the snow would be out
    on River Road,
how many minutes we had before it grew dark.

Trying to Tell My Mother
about Her Guardian Angel

When my mother stared out the blank
    window
I started to talk about her guardian
    angel,
the one assigned to her at birth
who would protect her from all harm,
his wings spread wide on her either side
so she'd be safe to walk down to Rosa's
    and buy her five tomatoes,
lift the watermelon and weigh it on the
    silvery scale like the other mothers.
I took out the blue book Sister had given
    me to bring
home, showed her the Mighty One with peacock
    wings and a flaming sword,
the thousand eyes staring back at both of us
    in that third-
floor flat as September's darkness came on,
    the one who slew the Giant Serpent,
God's own right hand who had cast Satan into hell,
and I saw my mother's eyes narrow, mirrored
    in that gray window
where cars drifted and electric wires trembled,
I watched her knuckles whiten on the sill

while the Black Angel stirred in her black heart,
    rising up,
as we had been told in that first-grade class,
    in great wrath,
and I knew even the Four Angels of Light could not
    save me,
whispering their names under my breath,
listening for the whish of their six seraphic wings
    in that silence
when she turned and wrapped her white arm
    around my neck.

Second-Grade Angel

Each choir had 6,666 legions,
with 6,666 angels in each of these
and I knew as sure as the fluorescent
    light
in that second-grade class kept blinking
that I had been one of them, still was,
    but sent
to earth because of some unforgivable
    sin,
that all I had to do was lift the window
and I could soar out onto Ontario Street,
    wings
erupting from my shoulders, the white
    shirt
tearing off, the school's striped tie
and gray trousers floating away, and I knew
    I had fire
in my tongue, my right hand filled with
    lightning,
that Sister Maria must have seen it
    but decided
to keep quiet so the others wouldn't bow
    down to me and lose their places
as we pledged allegiance and recited
    the Commandments, the Mysteries,

the invisible wings on my either side telling me
   again
my true father was not a road man for the Golden
   Eagle bread company,
my mother not a textile stitcher who danced
   nights with drunks at Boney's,
knowing I could soar above the blue earth, up
   into the darkness
where my brother did not walk alleys calling
   for rags,
that dogs howled when I walked by because
   they sensed
the fire in my body, that the dates of my birth,
   3/13/50
added up to the magical number of 66
and gave me power over seasons and planets, able
   to make
Margaret Blake throw up because she tripped me,
giving Ronny Michaels the hiccups for shoving
   me down the stairs,
sure even then I would ascend again some day,
despite my heavy body, the warts on my hands,
and I would become who I was, and I would know
   my real name.

Holding Out the Hands

He'd hold out his hands and
  open them
to a gleaming marble or penny
  or basketball pin
if I could guess which fist
  was closed on emptiness,
that sinking feeling if fingers
  splayed the air
to show nothing, my brother Nick
able to make things disappear
and pull them out of his mouth, from
  behind
his ear, once, pulling down his pants
  in the kitchen
and pulling a long string out of his
  ass,
making me shout *Do it again, Do it again,*
  not knowing
he would enter madness within a year,
that he would fade into a picture
  of a young man
in green pajamas in a green corridor
  taped
for a while to my dresser mirror,
then put into the clear plastic
  sheath

of a photograph album only to be
   found
today, more than twenty years later,
   cold October,
where I hold my fists out above
   the table
to no one there, my thumbs curled
   outside the fingers
the way he'd taught me to throw
   a punch,
thinking about swinging and jabbing
   the air
but knowing that wouldn't help,
holding them there, tight, whitening,
waiting for someone to guess which one.

Near the Paulite Church

For the first six months I did not know
    the bells
were clanging me to mass at seven, twelve,
    and again at eight,
their uneven tolling waking me from sleep,
    from books, from dark.
I would have gone on November first,
the day my father swung at the Black
    Angel
on his chest but missed, dying seconds
    later of a weak heart;
I would have knelt on Christmas Eve
    and February thirteenth,
to celebrate Christ's birth and my son's
    birth, would
have prayed and dropped bills into the
    basket
for a God I'm not sure exists, offered
    up my black days
to the staked saints that flared in Sunday's
    blood-red flames,
muttering *Mea culpa, Mea culpa* to the clumped
    rag my mother still held
before my eight-year-old face. But
I am not worthy of the small wooden cross

my brother fingered smooth until his death in madness,
    nor the Gospel lines my friend David sends.
On an ordinary Tuesday I bow my head. Nothing
stirs. I don't know who or what is dead.

Joey McGraw's Desk, 1960

As Sister Ann Zita asked the name
   of the longest river
in the world, or the capital
   of France, how
many grams in an ounce, Joey
   McGraw
was always the first with his hand
   up, not
waving like the rest of us who may
   or may
not have known the answer, his arm
   rigid and straight
as the flagpole stuck in the heavy
   base
at the front of that seventh-grade
   class. *Slow*
Joe, we'd yell at recess when he hit
   the ball
and would stroll the bases because he
   did not want
to wrinkle his pants or get dirt on his
   starched white shirt,
Sly Joe those nights he danced
   in and out
of pastel circles with Big Tits Joanne,

always ending up behind the bleachers
    until
the lights came on. *Thin Joe* when
    he got cancer
and sat in the last seat by the window
    watching
the sparrows peck seeds from the gold
    turds
of the Freihofer's horse, still raising
    his hand
now and then to tell us the angles
    and degrees,
repeating the Seven Deadly Sins without
    stopping
for breath, but mostly carving small
    stick
figures into his desk with the black
    Boy Scout knife,
crooked hearts Sister did not yell
about, lines of numbers from top to
    bottom
he never added up, a giant swastika
    right in the middle
because his father had been at the Battle
    of the Bulge,
desk no one was allowed to sit in from
    January to June,
Marking his absence, Sister had said,
    as we filed

past it coming in, going out for lunch
    and recess,
trying to make sense those first few days
    of the figures he drew,
arguing about the small *x*'s, the word *sporadical*
    by the inkwell,
peering at the sticker of the Mack truck bulldog
    he'd put on the hood
of an Edsel, no mistake, we knew, but still
    unable
to figure it out as we walked home from school,
    dirty snow
clumps beginning to melt along the yellow curbs
that we tightrope walked as long as we could,
    wavering, arms out in the oncoming spring.

The Sparrow and
the Winter's Nest of Snow

Long winter day of cutting wood, old
    cherry trees
strangled by poison ivy, one a good
    three feet thick,
the trunk set aside for the lumber
    mill, the rest
cut up and stacked while I thought
of my distant son in his distant room,
of the full-page poems he sends in the mail,
    the winter's nest of snow
scribbled in his first-grade red and yellow
    and blue letters,
and the picture with each one,
huge oak trees and tiny daisies, always
    the sun in a blue sky.
And I remembered my father's drawings
    before he died,
how the sparrow came into each sketch,
sometimes on an arcing branch,
sometimes on a gutter,
the scruffy brown feathers and yellow-orange
    beak,
the tiny claws clasping whatever it was on,
sparrow with its small song,

sparrow indistinguishable from the winter's brown weeds,
sparrow of the mind of my father that has flown
    into darkness,
sparrow above the glass of Schaefer's, the pack of Luckies,
sparrow of the blackened heart and short-distance flight,
    sparrow of forty-seven years and a mad wife.
Sparrow darting now over my buzzing saw and bent head,
    making me look up
at the steel sky, upstate New York winter wind
    whipping my eyes,
poor, stupid sparrow in this five below,
searching for *the winter's nest of snow*,
sparrow stumbling down the streets of Cohoes
    mumbling Irene, Marjorie, Irene,
sparrow pulling out the racks of doughnuts, cakes
    and pies
those early mornings of the Golden Eagle bread route,
taking the iced curves in the road at seventy miles,
pock-marked, skinny, malarial-ridden, drunken sparrow,
I follow you a few seconds in this light, then let you go.

Written with my son, Joshua Roberts

21 ◆

When the angel finally came down

to one good man
and Lot could not find him, I
could only nod my head in the back
    of that sixth-grade class,
whisper *Yes, Yes* as my fingers
    twirled
Donna's gold hair around my yellow
    No. 2 pencil,
letting it roll down, curling it up
    again,
Donna not moving at all, me not
    knowing
if she felt the slight tug, the way,
    nights now,
I don't know what the woman I'm with
    thinks
when we make love, when she lays her head
    on my chest,
what words are forming in her dark,
where she's gone, where she's been,
watching my own scenes unreel
the way that pencil did back then
when I looked up to see the blackboard
    washed
completely clean by Barbara McGill,
    the arch

forming at the small of her back
as she stretched up, up into the black.

My wife wants me to cut

the black
walnut down because
    its leaves
drift into the pool
and leave dark-brown
    stains
on the smooth blue
    bottom,
especially in early
    autumn,
when it's still warm
    enough
to swim and the walnut
    sends
its dried, crinkled
    leaves
with any wind, at night
    hundreds
of curled shreds finding
    their way
to the clean concrete,
    leaving
their mark, their print
    so clear
in bold daylight that
    my wife

grows bitter in the sun's
    dying
slant of September, October,
    she whispers
in the heat of the electric
    blanket
that I must cut the dirty
    thing down,
its thin branches littering
    the lawn,
the heavy green pods that
    rot
all winter, burying them-
    selves
in the hardening ground,
    the brown
stain on my son's cheeks
a smear I swipe, she knows,
    every chance
I get, on my forehead, too,
    around our deep-
set eyes, three slashes on
    our necks,
drawing the yellow-brown
    bitterness
 in wavery circles around
    our hearts
that will not wash off.

Three Stars

As I hauled hay to the barn for
the horse and cow, I was stopped
by the violet and blue-gray clouds
    of Pennsylvania January
sunset, that cold-iron hue that flared
    up to end
the few clear days. The woods
were stripped and three stars glimmered
    behind the black branches,
two small yellow-white stars and one
    pale green,
the star of hope I'd come to look for
    these past four years. Turn
around three times when you first sight
    three stars, my crazy Indian
grandfather always said—although stars
    were hard to see on Olmstead Street—
and so I spun in the foot of snow to the
    sound of his voice and the hollow
wind which his voice had joined, my legs
    crossing the way his crossed
on the brown porch as he danced from light
    into dark. Dusk
is the sacred time of ghosts returning,
when souls appear to pursue their bodies
    and the harrowed of the world

stretch into below-zero cold their vast
    snow wings,
and I was there to watch them, more snow devils
    and snow angels
than I could count as they whirled off the barn
    roof,
and I no longer wanted to ask where they had gone,
    or what they did,
caught in those moments white and light as snow
that pass beneath these three dim stars.

Waiting for the voice or touch of God,

I counted the pink roses trellised
on the blue wall beside my head,
whispered the world's longest river,
the presidents' names,
the capitals and states,
afraid to stop, afraid to hang
my hand or leg over the edge
    of the bed
because I knew the Black Angel
    was there
ready to drag me in, that only
the angel on my right could hold
    me back
from becoming one of them, the
    daughters
of Lilith squatting above me in
    my sleep,
making me wake to a wet sheet,
    an Act of Contrition,
five Our Fathers, five Hail Marys
even as I rose to stare at the young
    girls
posed naked in my brother's second
    drawer,

Old Horny and Lusty Dick stamped
across their tops in red ink,
the Devil's footsteps in my left
　　ear
when I snuck downstairs to lift my
　　mother's underwear
from the wicker basket, run my
　　fingers
over the embroidered yellow daisies,
　　the blue iris,
begging forgiveness as I felt their
　　silk
and imagined her white body on top
　　of him,
heard their come-cries rise through
　　the tin ceiling,
making the sign of the cross
when I tiptoed back to bed
and felt the ashes of lust mound
　　in my blackened heart,
remembering the saint's command
to cut off the hand that would offend,
　　considering it
as I began to hum in that cold dark,
surprised at the lightness of my body,
　　the lightness of my voice.

Splitting Wood with Milton
and the Devils, Wassergass

Stacking the split walnut, maple,
    oak, and mulberry
in cold Pennsylvania January
I look up now and then
at the bare branches,
    remembering
they fell thick as autumn leaves,
    for nine days they fell,
wondering how long it took
    my father
to drop from Boney's Bar into St.
    Joseph's Cemetery,
how many minutes my mother had
    to drive
from the textile plant to her
    lover's
bed, counting up the number of sins
    I could commit
in nine full days and nights, whirling
    the ax
into the air at the thought of it,
    so many wings
and flaming tongues, so many cunts
    and tits

and lies they could easily fill this
    vast gray sky
where nothing stirs except the wind,
reminding me that, too, could be the
    demon's work,
seeing my right foot forward, the sign
    of the Dragon
of Dawn, waiting for the souls to descend
    in the bodies
of flies, my terrible separation from love
    reflected
in their myriad eyes, bringing back
that morning driveway where I waved good-bye
    and drove
into Ohio, into nonbeing and purposelessness,
the years bringing me here to this woodpile
    in Pennsylvania,
all flesh with the 90,000 Angels of Hell
    lewdly whispering
and at least half a cord of wood left to be
    split.

Part 2

Counting the Black Angels

When I looked up, I saw
  133,306,668,
the number of angels Satan
had taken with him into the dark,
leaving the number on the right,
  266,613,336,
to remain loyal to the Throne,
a good one-third who had spread
  their wings
and settled at the core
where fire burned forever
  the soul of my father,
the dark man who had spent hours
  drinking at Boney's Bar,
and I knew my mother would join
  him
there for leaving with the fat
  Irishman,
that I would have to cut off my
  hand
so it wouldn't keep reaching to
  Karen Awlen's
pigtail whisking my desk, I would
  have to tie
a crucifix to my penis to stop it
  from rising

nights with naked women on top of
    me, their breasts
dangling the way Sister Maria's beads
    dangled
from her black robe when she swayed
    down the aisle
until I had to turn away, look out
the window to where snowflakes
    fell so thickly,
so swiftly I could not even hope
    to give them the names
of the Black Angels, Apollyon,
the Angel of the Bottomless Pit,
    Sammael, the
Poisonous One, Belial, Most
    Worthless,
and Maestema, the Accusing Angel
who pointed right at me through
my half-formed face in the window
    and whispered
Ann Harding, Ann Harding, Irene
    in her blue
bathing suit, the one who saw
the nights I stared into the dark
    of Olmstead Street's alley
hoping to see Lorraine's mother
    take off her bra,
Maestema, who saw me offer
    Michelle
a nickel for one little feel,
    who tangled

my fingers in her thick hair
that dusk at West Side Park,
dogs barking because they knew
I was a black angel, too, one
   of the fallen
into fires of lies and lust,
one who snuck out those hot summer
   nights
to sit on the back porch where I
   smoked forbidden cigarettes
and opened the June 1962 *Playboy*
   centerfold,
felt the seven serpent heads
   root
in my skin, one for each night
   of the week,
felt the black wings erupt
   from my shoulders,
forming the scalloped shadows I could
   show no one else
and so tucked under t-shirts and sport
   coats,
binding them for months with the
   incense
of St. Bernard's Church, hearing
them rustle and snap when lovely Mary
   walked to the board
to draw the chambers of the heart,
keeping silent, not saying a word
as they lifted me, weightless, resolved
   into the dark.

Walnuts

Clear October, the goldenrod and aster
   turned
from summer, Farewell to Summer
   already
having said farewell, and I raked
   the walnuts down
to the gravel driveway, so our car tires
   would crush
the thick, green shells and we could crack
   them open
on the blue porch, pick out the meat
   and eat.
I lifted them up and smelled their bitterness,
I smeared the brown walnut stain on my fingertips
   and thought
of my mother's walnut coffee table, her kitchen
   table and chairs, the rich,
dark brown of the walnut box she kept
   her fake pearl
necklace and earrings in. And I knew again
my mother would be dead within the year, by
   the time
new walnuts had once more grown full and fallen,
   her voice
thin as walnut stems, her hair sparse as the
   few walnut tree's leaves

that hung onto the black, twisted limbs,
and there, behind them, the cold clear
blue of winter coming.

Gift Shop in Pécs, Hungary

They paint yellow and red flowers
    on the white vases,
with pale green leaves and stems,
some with dark blue centers,
three dark blue circles with x's.
The embroidery, too, and the small
    carved walnut boxes,
flowers jutting out everywhere, not
    one Jew on the train
to Auschwitz, which is not so far
    from here,
not one young wife with two children
    dragged from her side. And
African masks, the death mask, the
    life mask, the mask
of love chiseled in jade-like stone,
so heavy I could hardly pick it up
to see the naked bodies, the veils
    covering and uncovering
them. I almost bought the many-armed
    Lady from India, the Wise Fool
from Vietnam, I almost paid the full
    thousand forints
for the handmade Polish moccasins
    with the pointed toes

and small beaded white horses, smaller
    men with sabers drawn
as they rode off the stitched edges.
I had to lift them all to feel their weight,
I had to bring them close so I could see
    the tiny hands and feet, the
curve of an arm, the straight nose, the
    buckle on his shoe, the gilly-
flower on hers, I had to feel the heaviness
    of their dreams, the foolishness
of their hopes as they dipped black bread
    into the bowls, as they
snuffed out the candles name by name
by the tiny carved altar. I had to bend
    to hear their silence
as they bowed from the waist and curtsied,
    stiff-legged, without
a single moan, not one face turned
    away, not one hand raised
as they began their strange dance
    on the dustless shelves.

Learning Animals and
Insects in Third Grade

I could hear the horse neigh in that
    third-grade class,
its big head poked over the picture's
    white picket fence
while Sister told us the old, useless
    ones were sent to Alpo
or Zweiger's Glue Factory on Cherry Road,
each of us looking around to see if it was true,
seeing all kinds of snakes sloughing their skins
and bats hanging by their claws in the dark
    caves underground,
a giant turtle on its back, gasping for breath
as we sat straight at our desks
and yelled out which ones lay eggs,
which ones bore their young, listening
to the whales as they circled the globe,
listening to Ray Martineau's asthmatic breathing
that fell like the falling snow, *shhhh, shhhh,*
    against the dripping window,
one of every kind of beast circling us,
all their eyes mirroring our eyes back
except for the ants who never stopped tunneling
    into their glass-caged earth,

busy from the second our lights went on
with their tunnels that went sideways and up
    and down,
sudden small pockets of silence in which they
    passed
along the shadowed, erratic trails that dead-ended
    against invisible walls
and then doubled back, again and again, in that
    late, upstate New York winter day.

The Cowboy

In that dim parlor I strapped
   on
the gleaming white double holster
   with a red
gem in the buckle's center, cinched
   the leather
strings to each thigh, rolled
   the cylinders
to be sure I had a rubber
   bullet
in each hole, ready again
to walk into the darkness
   of the
closet my mother had said
   I must sit
in for an hour, her hands
   mottled
on the windowsill as I
   strode in spurs
across the green carpet,
my back stiff as I could
   make it,
my white hat tipped down
   over
eyes I would not let her
   see,

even when she said I did
   not
have to go in there, if
   I'd give
her a kiss, say I was sorry,
as rigid then as I am today,
   my breath
clamped inside my body,
every cell of me trembling
as I opened the door and clicked
   into that dark.

Lee's Chinese Laundry

for Gus Pelletier

Even then they were toothless, grinning,
    ancient faces
floating above white robes that shone
    so brightly
in that Remsen Street sun I had to
    shade
my eyes, the oldest of them pointing
    at me
and saying *the Wone Wanger,* all the
    others
bowing their heads to the steaming irons
    on long wooden boards,
their pigtails dangling along their necks,
    their ears,
shadows farther back looking like women
    with wings
that dipped and rose again and again,
    flowing
into buckets of water one would then lift
    and throw
out the opened, gleaming door even as
    young Lee
lifted me onto the counter to teach
    me how to keep

the metal balls clicking on the thin
    stick,
showed me the black kimono with gold and
    red dragon
threads, the head reared back, dragon
    smoke flowing
into my breath, his quick fingers making
    houses and trees and sunsets
into words I slowly began to comprehend,
    believing
I could become one of them, sleeping
    in rows
along the walls where they woke to work,
    taking small,
precise steps, our voices in a rise and fall
like the songs of sparrows lined up on the
    backyard fence, facing north
into the cold, glittering autumn wind.

After the Second Operation

This time when I woke from the
    anesthesia
I heard myself mumbling words
    from
a poem I had written for my son,
not like a year ago when I'd come
    to
fumbling after an old nurse's ass,
telling her we could have some fun,
    thinking
in that daze she was lovely
    Lorraine
curled in the back seat of the '59
    Chevy,
that I had just unsnapped her bra
    and lifted
her tattooed breasts to my lips,
    kissed
the rose unfurled around one nipple,
an inch-high cardinal hovering above
    the other,
but in truth I'd been strapped
to a rolling cart, my nose broken,
    my throat
stitched, needles in my arms dripping
    while my wife

and son walked on my either side,
    me looking up
now and then as though I'd wanted
    to talk,
forming words I knew they could
    not
understand, my hands lifted a few
    inches
from the cool rails, as high as I
    could stretch
them, fingers splayed as though
    signaling
while I was rolled, nodding, down
that fluorescent-lit, yellow-gray
    hallway.

My Father's Fence

My father started to paint the beer
  bottles
white and stuck them in the rusted
  holes
of the fence at all angles, mouths
  down, mouths
sideways or up, catching the wind
  the way
he liked, he said, a slow moaning
  drifting
those nights to where I slept,
  window
open to the riffs of the beer
  my father
had drunk, to the women who groaned
  on his creaking bed,
a whole orchestra out there
bordering our ten-by-ten-foot
  backyard
and the dusty alley, even the
  cats
staying away, the dogs howling
  down
by Tremblay's once the bottles
  started

to play, old man Ouimet shouting
  Shut up!
to the wind's blowing over
  emptiness,
Porky and Junior shattering
  them
with pellet shot, lovely Irene
  telling me
one dusk as we talked over the
  trembling
fence that she knew they would
  bring us
good luck, asking me in her
  softest voice
if she could come in
through the rickety gate
that clanked and moaned and
  thrummed
when it opened up.

Shrinking as they rise, the

constellations
grow so much smaller late at night
when I walk softly out of the house,
trying not to wake anyone up,
sitting here on the blue porch
to see Cassiopeia the size of a book-
    end,
Draco the Dragon smaller than
    a milksnake,
realizing again I am shrinking,
the picture taken last month in which
    my son
rises above my head
so much like the one
taken of me and my father as we stood
    in front of St. Bernard's,
my graduation diploma in my folded hands,
his pockmarked face looking into my neck,
my padded shoulders level with his bloodshot
    eyes,
and I know the bells were ringing
and the people all around us were laughing and
    loudly talking,
that cars swished by in the afternoon sun
but I just looked down on my father's waved hair,

smelled the Schaefer's on his dark breath,
refusing to shake his hand which even now
holds itself out, twenty-three years after
    his death,
into this clear-night December Pennsylvania air.

Emma in the Class on Reproduction

Ronny Michaels would go blind,
Richie Fremont grow hair on his palms,
Maureen Risteau's and Sylvia Ryan's
bellies grow big as beach balls
if we did not heed the Messenger
    of the Lord,
his wings outstretched in that seventh-
    grade classroom
where Sister Ann Zita drew testicles
    and vaginas on the board,
the condom passed from desk to desk
    to show us what it was like,
Ann Harding holding it at arm's length,
Donald Wilcox trying to blow it up
while the rest of us stared at the outlined
    man and woman
on the wall-sized print, the dotted lines
of the penis inside the dotted lines of the *cunt,*
word Johnny Dumas whispered from the back,
making us look up, making us laugh.
This is not funny, Sister said, whacking
    the thick pointer in her palm,
staring at Ronny and Donald, at easy Emma
who spread her knees at lunch and showed her
    underpants,

Emma, the girl the high school boys took
    to the Cliff,
the Cohoes Drive-In, to the after-midnight
    parties at Charrette's,
lovely Emma who wore a black bra beneath the
    white blouse,
who never tucked in her legs or hitched up
    her skirt,
who dyed her hair blond, then red, then
    streaked
it silver and brown, who wore a heavy gold
    heart
between her breasts and smeared gold specks
    on her lips
that Father Mulqueen always wiped off at the Front
    Street entrance. Emma,
who raised her hand that day to ask Sister
    how she knew about love
and was made to stay after school for a month
    in detention,
writing a thousand times, *I am sassy and bold*
    in red ink,
then having to do it all over again in blue,
Emma, who walked in one day with giant wings
tied to her arms and declared she was our angel,
Emma, whose cheeks flared with the flames
    of Sister's fingers,
whose hands bled from welts ridged by Sister's
    triangular ruler,

who was made to sit on a stool in front of the class
while we learned about syphilis and crabs and gonorrhea,
how a virgin bled, how a woman bled every month,
Emma's heart-shaped face white as the chalked words
     drifting
in blurred clouds on the board behind her,
     love, abortion, marriage, sex
as she wet her lips with her pink, pink tongue.

Talking with God

Those nights God would talk
   to me
it was always in someone else's
   voice,
my grandmother's early morning
   murmur
when she threw down the apple or
   pear,
the Three Musketeer candy bar,
asking what I did last night,
or Monsignor Mulqueen's whispering
   Some
boys had broken windows in the
   condemned
building next door, Could I know
   who it was?
Irene in the shed behind Desormau's
   taking down
one strap of her bra, telling me
   she saw
Sherri sitting beside me in the last
   row
of the Cohoes Theater on Saturday,
   What was that all about?
and I found myself talking back,

the way I still do today, walking
  through the fields
as I pick aster and chickory and
  late
daisies for the cracked blue vase,
saying *Yes, it was me,* or *No, that
  was Junior
or Porky or Gary,* holding my hands
  up
to show there's nothing in them
  but
wildflowers, unbuttoning my fall
  coat
to show there's nothing in my heart
  except
a few old cars, a brocaded dress,
  one dead cat
turning on a spit, my younger brother
  crying
in the cold hallway as I held him
  down
with my knees on his arms and slapped
  his red
face, the woman swallowing pills one
  afternoon
looming up in the goldenrod, the unborn
  one
floating away in a plastic bag among
  the gathering
clouds, mumbling as I do these nights
  in my

sleep, *See, see,* buttoning up again
  because
it's cold and there are so many more
  flowers to pick,
watching the sky for signs, trying
to keep my eyes on the hardening ground.

Bringing Ziggy His Homework
after the Accident

After supper I'd bring him
   the assignments
of addition and loss, the
   blue maps
of the the world where he
   had to mark
the names of oceans and
   continents,
his one hand crawling so slowly
   across
the colored paper I had to stare
at the metal vest around his back
   and chest
glowing in that dim parlor,
the two braces on his legs
   turning
him into a robot that could not
   budge from the green chair,
his head nodding above the white
   collar
of his neck when I asked if he wanted
   a glass
of water, hoping he would not choke

as I told him about lovely Lorraine's
    beginning
breasts, how Al Bouchard had dropped
    three frogs
out the fourth-story window onto the
    nuns' heads,
whispered the pink shade of Ann Harding's
    underpants,
the flowers along their laced edge,
that Ronny Michaels claimed he'd un-
    buttoned
her blouse while she babysat at the
    Reeses' house,
our eyes meeting when I repeated
    how Ronny
said her breast just popped out,
    the nipple
so long and hard he could roll
    it between
his finger and thumb, Ziggy raising
    his good
hand to mimic it in front of my eyes,
first clockwise, then counterclockwise.

Clear January, zero degrees, my last

    day in that state's
winter, and I knelt at my father's
    cold stone
the way he knelt in St. Bernard's pews,
    hungover, limp
with the stink of drunk Irene flooding
    him, the jungle
rot holes of his face glistening
in the stained-glass light as he breathed
    the incense deeply
and sorted out for the thousandth-
thousandth time, *This is wrong, This is right.*
    He rose,
a meek, a pardoned sinner,
no more fights in Boney's Bar,
no more hour-long bottles of liquor,
no more horses at Saratoga, throwing
    the stubs
on the heads in front of him, no more
    cursing
the horse, the horse's mother and father,
the gold initials of his ivory cuff links
flashing as he dropped the crumpled dollar
into the floating basket, his last buck,
he half-whispered, half-sighed, his beer
    breath clouding

my face, his bloodshot eyes
glinting the pastel light of saints into my eyes,
his bony hand on my shoulder making me lighter
    than I'd ever been, making me rise
beside him in that last pew in the corner
    of the church,
waiting for Maureen Risteau and her mother
    to click
down the aisle in their Sunday best,
both of us praising the Lord when they clicked
    their way back,
statue-white faces and arms, white gloves,
    white hats with black mesh,
pearl necklaces glistening in that early
    Sunday morning light
about their white, white necks.

Her Garden

Out there my mother's three
    spindly
tomatoes hung from their
white, bandaged sticks,
where she would kneel in dusk
before the tiny cucumbers, the
    thin heads
of lettuce, whitewash the ugly
    stones and set
them in a border that kept
nothing in or out, rocks
I stared at from my second-
    story window
those nights her voice rose,
    his
drifted off, and I wished
    I could toss
her out of that house into
    the street,
completely naked, no money,
no black and white polka dot dress
she wore with the fake pearl earrings,
    the fake pearl necklace,
no shiny black high heels she clicked
her way around that kitchen in,

whispering her name while I spit
the fifteen or so feet down
    onto her garden
as long as I could draw up
the thick wads of phlegm.

The Coin Trick

Good one, he whispered when the dime
  disappeared behind
my ear or I pulled it from my mouth,
my shirt pocket or jeans cuff,
holding it up as proof of the magic
  he'd taught me,
that quick reach into darkness where
  nothing had been
and then the gleam beneath the kitchen's
  dim bulb. *Good one,*
Good one, he'd whisper again, afraid
to wake the woman asleep in his bed,
clapping his small hands without a sound,
  the beer stink
of his breath drifting to where I clinked
  the coins
onto the table to show the positions
of Guam, of Guadalcanal,
three of them lined side by side for the
  Panama Zone, a quarter
for his brother's grave, another
for the green bathtub brimmed with ice
  to break his malarial fever,
a dime for our empty flat in Cohoes,
a nickel for my brother, his son,

who walked Albany's Veterans Hospital's
    green halls, pennies
for the others I tried to name before
    he swept
them into a mound and started flipping
    to see
how they'd land, calling out heads or
    tails as though
it mattered when he slapped them
into my waiting hand.

The Way of the Cross

When Sister said God was unknowable
    and unknown,
that only silence could express
    His Nothingness,
we hushed for a few seconds
in that sixth-grade class,
Joey McGraw, up front, white shirt,
    tie, pants pressed,
nodding his head, as though he could
    hear Him,
and Leslie Stiles, tall, blond girl with
    pimples
who carried the nuns' lunch from the
    convent,
sitting with her mouth open as though
    waiting
for God to soundlessly enter, Richie
    Freeman and Donald Wilcox
cocking their ears as they bet
    on an ant
that crawled past their desks,
Richie stomping down when it turned
    back,
making me laugh even as Sister wafted
    up the aisle

with the three-edged brass ruler, tapping
   heads as she went,
Good, Good, Good, she said till she got
   to where
I sat, then hissed *Bad, Bad,* and whacked
   till I bled,
the rosary beads on her belt clicking
   between
her knees, the silver cross on her chest
   thumping
while she shouted, *This is what happens
   to sinners,*
stumbling her way back to the front of the class
where she wrote *The Way of the Cross* with red chalk,
   told us
we must lift our crosses *up, up,*
so the sinner among us *might, might,* she whispered,
   get into heaven,
making us stand to do it that very second,
twenty-two eleven-year-olds lifting heavy crosses
   of air onto our shoulders,
balancing them there as we staggered around
   the empty seats,
some bumping into the scarred desks,
some easing them from shoulder to shoulder,
some stopping to kneel and catch their breath,
no one daring to put down the crossed weights
   or whisper a joke
as we circled each other for a silent hour
   that gray, darkening, December day.

My son insisted

we walk up the three hills to pick
chickory and aster and even goldenrod
   that he is
allergic to, so we could fill the blue
   vase set
every October on the round table,
calling me out of the house from the
   driveway,
the patio, the woodpile, the barn,
   his voice
everywhere out there under the falling
   walnuts
and gray clouds, his words floating
   between
the certain thuds of dropping pods,
Hurry up, we don't have much time
   before
it grows dark, Get a load on, Dad,
   What's
the matter, you got piss in your blood?
when I walked out with a jacket on, making
   me turn
back into the house to throw it over the
   couch,
feel the cold rush of air on my bare arms
   and neck

as we walked up the green road, him running
   ahead, then
back, then ahead again, holding up the
   papery
praying mantis sac, the abandoned
   nest,
the crumbling beehive he'd found in the
   crotch
of the blue spruce, telling me about the
   checks
he'd gotten in school, three in a week
   and if he
received two more he'd have to see
   the principal,
proud of his status as a near criminal,
   the sunset's
red in his new eyes, on his freshly washed
   hair
I bent down to smell, draw his scent in
   even
as he whirled off into the overgrown field,
   his head
barely above the dried grass that swished
   and grew
dead silent whenever he stopped.

Learning Natural Instincts

Giraffes munched leaves from the tops of trees
    on a plain in Africa
and eagles wheeled about a mountain nest
while my penis stiffened in that seventh-
    grade class,
Ann Harding's nipples dark beneath the white
    blouse,
Karen Awlen's thighs so white while hippos
    wallowed in mud
and I could only think of the last row
    in the Cohoes Theater
where I would sit on Sunday with Sherri,
my fingers twirling her long, red hair,
offering her jujube fruits and buttered
    popcorn for a kiss,
sliding my hand down her shoulder, brushing
    her breast,
her white body leaning into mine until
    Sister called me up to the front
to tell how the bat found its way in the dark,
how turtles knew when and where to lay their eggs,
Sister, who made me stand despite my instant
    bellyache,
despite the lump in my pants my penis made,
my mind racing for answers as the others pointed
    and laughed,

sonar, instinct, just plain dumb luck
    blurting out of my mouth
as I thought of cats flattened on the road,
of Margaret, my classmate, whose bones shone
    through her cancerous skin
when she rose every morning to throw up
into the black bucket of sawdust, but
knowing even then nothing would help,
not rosary beads nor prayers nor the sign
of the cross Sister made over my head,
knowing I was going to hell as she sent me back
    to my seat,
following the path God had cut in my brain,
following the tunnel God had dug in my heart.

Part 3

Looking up,

I see
they have nailed my father to the
great blue spruce, his bottles
   of Schaefer's clacking
in the wind, his breadman's purse
hanging stiffly in these below-
   zero degrees.
And behind him, on the white pine,
my mother in the blue bathrobe, her
   arms spread
wide as though embracing the air,
   her lips red
as the blood on her hands, her feet.
And I am there, too, shouting to
   my wife
who hangs from a tree seven or eight
   rows away
those words I didn't say, wanting
   to point
to the stars over the barn, where they
   appear in winter
Pennsylvania. And the little ones, too,
   tacked up
like life-sized dolls, twisting their
   heads and

jerking around because they haven't learned
    yet
how to be still, one shouting he wants to
    come down
because he hasn't learned to be silent yet,
    another crying
because he hasn't learned that won't help yet,
    another one, who
looks like my brother, starting to hum, which
may help some, but not much, in the crucified air.

It's All Right, It's OK

For three years now I have not
    visited
my father's grave up there
on the bare hill in St. Joseph's
    Cemetery,
passing within fifteen miles
    each December
but never turning off onto River
    Road
and along the Hudson till the
    Y,
the right branch leading me there,
    although
I can hear him calling me at
    a certain
point on the Northway, his voice
    with a limited
range, like the radio, a bit of
    static, then
clearing, when he says *It's all
    right, it's*
OK, the way he did those nights
    I'd come
home to him drunk, sprawled on the
    kitchen

floor, puke on his clothes, and
    I'd lift
him into the white tub, turn the
    cold
water on, consciousness flooding
    him
with the memory of his wife gone,
    jobless,
waving me away even then so I
would not, he mumbled, see him
    like this,
no trick coins to pull out of his
    mouth or ear,
no harmonica riff or quick tap
    dance,
just his beer-bloated body adrift
in water flecked with bits of pink
    vomit.

Killing Jesus

When Sister told us we had all
    killed Jesus,
spitballs driving the spikes
through his ankles and palms,
    forgetting
to genuflect before the statue
    of Mary
in the corridor shoving one more
    thorn
into his head, I saw the clumped
    rag
my mother held up to the bathroom
    light
as she told me I was making her bleed
    to death,
heard my father slam the door those
    late Friday nights
he dropped the white envelope of bills
    onto the table
and sighed, his pockmarked face
and beer-bloodshot eyes soon to be
    mine, I knew,
his skinny arms and legs, his blackened
    heart
growing inside me even as I studied

the green continents and blue oceans,
memorized the presidents and their dates,
 snapping
out 56 and 225 the split second the flash
 cards
appeared in Sister's hand, spelling
 bologna
and *mischievous* and *fluorescent,* the last
 to be set
down, ready to go on as long as someone
 asked
the quotient, the remainder, the Apostles'
 names, the Cardinal
Virtues, hoping somehow that knowledge
might lift me above Donald Wilcox turning
 the cat, howling,
on the fiery spit by the railroad tracks,
that the three books I read every week
 might make me worthy,
my head crammed with rivers that snaked,
 named,
through every one of my nights and days,
tagging the leaves ironed in waxed paper,
the planets that whirled in the slightest
 breeze,
knowing that water must flow on the skin
 to be baptized properly,
not sure the words were said correctly
 over me, three times, circling,

unable to understand my dark joy at my
   father's broken
drunkenness, my mother's window-staring
   madness,
the moments of clarity as I sat in the
   last
desk in the last row of that class, when
   I knew
if I were at the Crucifixion, I would be
   the one
with the lance, lifting it into the air
while the others repeated the speed
   of light
and sound, the distances of stars,
that I would not just rip a gash
   in Christ's side,
but would thrust up under the ribs
   to find His godly heart.

Love on Lonesome Drive Road

I can't rembember the necklaces or
    earrings
she wore, only the rings, amethyst,
    diamond,
pearl, and the charm bracelet with
    the neighing
horse, the silver house, the silver
    heart
that jangled as she jerked me off
    on Lonesome Drive Road,
knowing the Hudson River flowed
    somewhere
in front of us, the doors locked,
the windows steamed from our kissing,
    her breasts
popped out above her still-clasped
    bra,
half a submarine sandwich on the dash,
    a bottle
of Coke, the gold sparkle on her eyelids
    and lips
glittering in the little light, White
    Shoulders
enveloping us both as she stroked
    and I came
into the initialed handkerchief

she held snug with her left
    hand,
folding it neatly a few seconds
    after we were done,
dropping it into the white, pearly
    bag
she then clicked shut.

Pathways

Wondering if I've ever been truly
     penitent
for my sexual sins (impure
thoughts, desires, as well
     as touch),
I split logs into chunks for
     next
winter's fire, maple, beech,
     walnut, oak,
mulberry my favorite, brilliant
     yellow
in all this dull Pennsylvania
     January gray,
still unsure whether there's a
     God,
leaning into the north wind
the way I lean into belief,
     just so far,
it will, it won't, hold me up.

                  ◆

Cut out a large piece of black
     construction paper, then
punch holes or other patterns in it,
     letting

your hand move of its own accord,
Richie Freeman stabbing gashes with his
    scissors,
Ann Harding putting pinpricks in straight
    lines,
me afraid to even lift the X-ACTO knife
    my father used
for his layout and design class
at the local community college,
after his ten hours on the road
of the Golden Eagle bread route,
after the two quarts of Schaefer's gold,
    the knife I stole
with a few coins from his breadman's purse
when I thought he slept in the dark,
    the glitter of it
there in that fifth-grade class
where we held our lives up to the buzzing
    light
and mine was black, black, black.

    ◆

Pry bar, cat's claw, me
    up
over fifty feet in my life,
    on barn
ridge to tear off crumbling
    slate
 the same blue-gray of sky,
    mirror

within mirror in below-zero
   degrees, no
sane man out here in north
   wind, asking
Power/Creator/Death-Giver
   to hold off
on my young son, take me
   instead
any time, liver, heart, tumor
   in brain
no matter, leaving chicken ladder
   behind
to show Him/Her I'm not kidding,
   standing
high, one foot on either side,
arms out like wings, wavering.

     ◆

Reading last night how leaves
   grow
into auras of leaves photographed
   time
before, the form already there,
I put down the book to go look
   at stars,
clear December thousands of them
   in a cold black,
stood there on brick and half-
   brick
weave porch I laid last summer,
   pattern

Nancy and I talked back and forth
    about
for hours, unaware
of the Great Design,

                in them, in us.

    ◆

One moment in the field all moments
    popped
into my head, made me think I'd read
too much Chinese poetry, yet there it
    was,
one moment long as the field was long,
rippling up in the clarity of cold
like a wave, like the gong of a bell,
like the fat groundhog sleeping fast
    in his frozen hole,
like the end of the Fourth of July
    fireworks
in Hellertown which they hold on
    July 11th
to dissuade strangers from out of town,
    a fusillade, a barrage
of colors and forms splayed against the
    black sky,
lingering a moment on the mind's eye
    after they're gone.

    ◆

My son says *I love you, Dad,*
    I love you, Mom,

and tears well my eyes the way
    they do
when the townspeople put their
    money
into a basket for George near the
    end
of *It's a Wonderful Life,* when
    I pretend
to cough so Nancy and Josh won't
    know
I'm crying, being the Father, the
    Man
of the House, learning this when
I was younger than my son.

     ◆

Two warmish days sandwiched
    by below-zero
degrees and already the fat,
    black, hairy
flies were back, so slow I
    could catch
them in my hands, twenty-five
    feet up
on the ladder, re-tacking
    chicken wire
to the barn's window eave
    where starlings
come in to shit over every-
    thing. *Are*

you a soul? I asked one held
between forefinger and thumb,
    hearing
its buzz as I crushed its shell,
sent it back into hell.

♦

How long? What road? I ask in the cold
    December field
as I snip and lop and saw the branches
    that have doubled
back on themselves, the ones grown
    straight up
into the center where there must be
    light,
remembering my old friend telling me
    a bird could fly
through the limbs of a properly pruned
    tree
without touching wood or bud, stepping
    back
now and then to imagine that,
shaping the form of the tree
with that bird in mind.

♦

So this is it, free
of the past, those old bones
    and rings

within rings, a silver house,
   a silver horse
on a charm bracelet lost
on a wrist that's lost,
letting the too-wide paisley tie
and ivory tiepin and cuff links go,
the black and white polka-dotted
   dress,
like those late Saturday afternoons
   when I stepped
out of the confessional, the whish
   of the purple
curtain drawn aside for a few
   seconds
in which I was lifted up.

◆

Coldest days, and
I am heartily sorry for my sins,
*Mea culpa, Mea culpa, Mea maxima
   culpa*
on my lips as I tag white and red
   pine,
blue and Norway spruce, a few
   fir
with fluorescent pink ribbons,
   marking
those that have to be trans-
   planted
so the others can grow to full
   height, width,

searching my heart for some wrong
    I've done,
more than the number of evergreens
    in this six-acre field,
more than the number of needles
that quiver at this true end
    of the year.

Learning the Stars

Giant blue stars, yellows, and smaller reds
    whirled
across the seventh-grade blackboard
to form a flying horse and dogs, dippers,
Andromeda chained to a sea rock, Perseus's belt
cinched tight as Ann Harding's black patent leather strap,
Ronny Michaels whispering to Karen Awlen that he'd like
    to show her the stars from Canal Road,
Richie Reese staring off into space,
the braces on his legs wobbling as he clacked
to the board to circle the three stars of Polaris,
    Castor's six,
reciting the light years' distance to Antares,
telling us the ancients believed they were ruled
    by the stars
before he hobbled back to his desk.
    Alpheratz, Algol, Capella,
stars we traced and cut out on stiff
    construction paper,
brushed with fluorescent paints,
stars I carried home and set like sequins
    on my bedroom ceiling,
imagining the lines that made them figures
    I could comprehend
when I lay sleepless, my older brother's
    madness

glowing beside me in a cluster of light,
my younger brother jerking off every night,
red Aldebaran gleaming down on us from
    the Bull's eye
as I wrapped myself in the black cloak
    which made me invisible,
the Pole Star burning where my heart had been,
each star a cell in my space-darkened body,
star trails crisscrossing even then from my mind
    to my balls,
my fingers burning, my eyes burning in that field
    of flames,
the Star of Betrayal marked in ash on my forehead,
the Star of Hope flickering in my throat
where the names took shape in the absence of space,
    Harp, Bow, Sailing Ship,
pinpoints of light I could travel by, clear, bright,
    and fixed.

He's Alone

He's alone in St. Joseph's Cemetery under the common stone.
He's not cold although it's ten below, I know, I've stood
   there many a winter day, but not any more.
He's alone like the nights he rocked through the dark, his
   lit cigarette a red coal rising and falling
while he practised for what he does now for all eternity.
The holes in his face are gone, fallen into themselves. Now
   the holes in his bones are going.
His quick fingers and receding hairline and silent tongue
   and dirty cock, as my mother screamed it, are gone too.
There's not much left up there on the bare hill with no
   trees,
where the snow drifts against the stone and covers the name,
   the dates, the etched
flowers that do not look like flowers.
He's finally all white in a complete black, alone with
   his glasses of Schaefer's, his Lucky Strikes,
his Guam, his Guadalcanal, his Panama Zone, his black books
   where naked women still sit on a long log, breasts
   hanging down, smiling into the camera.
He's alone with his harmonica which he stopped playing
   the last seven years of his life,
and with his perking coffee pot, the bubble bursting
   inside that clear glass dome,

his nine spoonfuls of coffee for the pot and one spoonful
    of salt for the bitterness,
the ivory cuff links with the glittering gold *R*'s
    that no longer glitter,
his hundred and five pounds at the end, his broken
    back, his damaged heart, his red eyes,
his awful habit of tailgating, of slamming on the brakes
    to skid over ice
while he whistled "Please Love Me Forever" or "The Other Side
    of the Mountain"
until the black wings landed on his chest, which he swung
    at but missed
as they carried him off.

The Tools

Cat's claw, pry bar, mallet and
   hatchet,
pick, hole-digger, ratchet, set of
   wrenches
and allen wrench, twelve-penny common
   and spike,
bird's mouth, anchor brace, gap,
my life for the past twenty-five
   years on the top
ridge of houses and barns, blue-
   gray sky
and slate, chicken ladder leading
   to heaven
and corrugated asphalt driven down
   with self-
sealing ringed nails, chainsaw snarling,
   exactly right mix,
through oak, elm, walnut, mulberry,
the ax, the wedge, dusk and snow,
   my sweat
sweet as blood sucked from the open
   slit
so many times of the utility knife,
taking the work boots off to soak
   feet

in a shallow blue pan, epsom salts
  while the bones
in my vertebrae realign themselves,
  snap back
so I can walk out on the patio
  I built, brick, half-
brick weave design and stare up at
  the old stars,
learning the time of the seasons
  and the constellations,
not worried that tonight it will
  drop
to ten below, the footer a full four
  feet down
and wider at the bottom, staying put
no matter how much the earth heaves.

Reconsidering the Commandments

I walk around mumbling *Thou*
    shalt,
Thou shalt not,
toning through the October
    air as I bend
to the marigold and zinnia,
the aster and chickory and
    goldenrod,
knocking their little heads
    like bells,
whiffing them in as though
they were censers swinging
    back
when we walked the Stations
    of the Cross,
purple shrouds on the statues,
purple crossed with gold
on the priest's flowing robe,
sin taking wing in that echoing
    church
as Sherri and Lorraine swayed
    in,
Irene and Jeannette tossing their
    hair
back in waves that come rippling
    to me

in this Pennsylvania field
with the long, dried grass,
White Shoulders and Jean Naté,
    Fay's
scent on my fingertips in the
    back
seat of the '62 Chevrolet,
    the huge
heart I drew on the fogged
    window
with our initials in the middle,
    the wavery arrow
that soared off into the drive-
    in night
even as it began to melt.

Rolling the World in St. Bernard's

Richie Freeman took three long strides
    and rolled
the world down St. Bernard's hall,
showing Donald Wilcox a curve
even though the globe did not have
    three holes
like Richie's bowling ball, the blue
    sphere
clacking on its equatorial line
    each time
it went over one of the cracks in the
    floor, arcing
from Sister Ann Zita's closed seventh-
    grade door
all the way down to Sister Julia's
    kindergarten
class where little kids lined up
    with red
and yellow and green leaves in their
    hands, one
of them seeing the rolling world and
    screaming
as it crashed into them, sent a few
    flying,
others buckling and tumbling until
    it was just

like Richie had said it would be, human
    pins scattering
every which-way, the world finally still,
    lost somewhere
in the center of that confused mass, only
    Monsignor
Mulqueen's swishing out of the principal's
    office
stopping our cheers and laughs, the
    cigar
dropping ash as he slowly walked toward
    the half-
circle we had formed to watch, Richie
    smack
in the middle, head bent, not able to
    stop
giggling until Monsignor slapped his
    cheek
hard, handing him the dented world
    without
a word, standing there in his un-
    buttoned frock,
his white t-shirted belly hanging
    over the black
belt, as though he were God.

In the Field

For years I've watched the flight
of birds, how they trembled branches,
    stalks,
and I've bent to examine
deer tracks, rabbit tracks,
looking for the secret message.
Ahead of me, once, on the path,
I saw my mother's white, white back,
and behind her, my dead brother
taking his gold watch and ring off,
slicking his hair back in a big wave
before he turned to kiss me at the frosted door.
My old friend out there, too,
naming the flowers and weeds, grumbling
about pissants and pills he took,
    talking to the gnats
who, he said, knew his bitter heart,
his poor eyes that saw death for miles around,
his poor ears still listening after fifty years
for the high school band that made him cower
in his Chicago attic every 6:30 a.m.
I did not ask which path was the way out,
    or where Jimmy Charette, who clutched
his heart just after his missed jump shot, was,
or Glenn Brust, blown apart by a mortar shell
    more than twenty years ago.

The poison ivy towered four feet tall,
the copperhead moved slowly in the leaves,
sliding just inches from my feet,
his small forked tongue sipping the air,
his black, beady eyes of unbeing brushing by me
as though I were not one of the living,
as though my heart and lungs and breath
did not separate me from the dead,
as though the young boy I had been had died
    and rotted inside,
his dead lips and eyes now mine,
his long-dead hands raised back then now mine,
that boy's nights of endless falling ending there,
in that field, that body, that knowledge.

November Riffs

I watch my five-year-old
   boy run up
the hill toward the blue
   slide shining
in the blue sky, and I
   jingle
coins in my pockets
the way my father did,
pluck the wheat stalk
and stick it between
   my teeth,
moving it in circles with
   my tongue,
as he did before the gray
   stone
with his misspelled name
and the dates I keep repeating,
   1922, 1969.
By the time I get to the stone
   row, the crows
are cawing from the three dead
   oaks,
my son hurls thick, green walnut
   pods
into the empty air where my father
   now lives

without women or booze or the nights
of rocking
on the cracked kitchen linoleum.
He is silent here, as he was there,
only the lifting wind playing a riff
from Tommy Edwards's "Please Love Me Forever,"
There was a girl drifting
from the north side of the hill,
his stockinged feet swishing with my son's feet
through
the dried, crinkled walnut leaves,
his jungle-rotted face now my son's faultless face,
his bloodshot eyes my son's clear eyes,
his heavy heart my son's bird heart
I feel pounding
as I lift him up and whirl him through the November dusk.

What Sins, Now

For weeks I've walked around with
   I am heartily sorry
on my lips, and I've tried to think
   what sins,
now, would bring this old phrase
   back
from the dark confessional where I
   would kneel
and tell all, the screen between
   Monsignor Mulqueen
and me never dark enough, trying
   to disguise
my voice, make it older so he
   would not go crazy
when I said I held Lorraine's
   breast,
eased off her flowered under-
   pants,
almost growling when I got
   to the part
of her jerking me off, not
   certain
I had to mention her tongue
   in my mouth,
just as I'm not sure today
where my wife has been

when she comes home three
    hours late,
what thoughts come back
    to her
as we lie in bed, asking
    in a voice
that is not my voice
if she's heard from her old
    boyfriend,
the one she'd sent the note
    to the year
our son was born, letter
    returned
with address unknown,
her voice not her voice
    as she says *No,*
of course not, Go to
    sleep,
her hand patting my hip
    as she turns
away, both of us breathing
    light
as we can, for hours like
    that,
with nothing else to say.

On Hearing That We Were All Boundless, Unimaginable Energy

In that fourth-grade class when I heard
    we were all boundless,
unimaginable energy packed into our small
    bodies,
I looked out at the snow falling
    and felt myself
beginning to freeze, I put my nose
    to the wet window
and breathed out what I thought to be
    my soul,
letting it become mist in which I drew
    my initials
inside a watery heart, a wavery arrow
piercing it with a triangular tip,
the last thing I saw before Sister Thomas
    hit
me with her pointed ruler, told me to stand
    before the class
with the white dunce cap balanced
    on my head, but
I was gone down Ontario Street into
    Garcia's music
as he sat, legless on the corner, playing
    the violin,

I rode on the blue blanket of the Freihofer's
    horse as it clopped
to the back door of town hall, I was set
    free
of my poor body being poked and laughed at
    by those other poor bodies,
Lorraine and Ann in their white blouses and
    plaid skirts,
Alfred with his three rings gleaming
while I returned to hover above Sister's
    head, became
the jaguar prowling the cork board behind her,
closing my eyes so no one could see the streaming
    rays of light,
keeping my hands balled so they wouldn't flow
    with heat,
tightly biting my lips so the words would not come
    out by which they might know me,
gulping them down, one by one, tasting the mist.

Ready in Wassergass

Remembering the man who cursed
    his father or mother
would surely be put to death,
    I imagined spikes
driven through my palms for those
    nights
I stomped up the stairs yelling
    she was a tramp,
a sword in my gut for the times
    I whispered
You're a drunk, get up and fight,
    C'mon, C'mon,
my back an ache for more than ten
    years now
because I shouted *Whore, Easy screw,*
because I told everyone I knew
    in Cohoes, New York
that she slept with a dark Irishman
    from Troy,
that he sobbed nights on the orange-
    flowered couch,
my eyes searching this frosted ground
    for the slow
copperhead because I still believe,
    as I did

in that childish bed, that someone was
  always
watching what I did, listening to what
  I said,
even as I give the finger to north and
  south,
east and west, letting whoever it is
  know
that I'm still here, shouting *Up yours!*
  and
Fuck you! ready for judgment.

Illinois Poetry Series
Laurence Lieberman, Editor

History Is Your Own Heartbeat
  Michael S. Harper (1971)

The Foreclosure
  Richard Emil Braun (1972)

The Scrawny Sonnets and
  Other Narratives
  Robert Bagg (1973)

The Creation Frame
  Phyllis Thompson (1973)

To All Appearances: Poems New
  and Selected
  Josephine Miles (1974)

The Black Hawk Songs
  Michael Borich (1975)

Nightmare Begins Responsibility
  Michael S. Harper (1975)

The Wichita Poems
  Michael Van Walleghen (1975)

Images of Kin: New and
  Selected Poems
  Michael S. Harper (1977)

Poems of the Two Worlds
  Frederick Morgan (1977)

Cumberland Station
  Dave Smith (1977)

Tracking
  Virginia R. Terris (1977)

Riversongs
  Michael Anania (1978)

On Earth as It Is
  Dan Masterson (1978)

Coming to Terms
  Josephine Miles (1979)

Death Mother and Other Poems
  Frederick Morgan (1979)

Goshawk, Antelope
  Dave Smith (1979)

Local Men
  James Whitehead (1979)

Searching the Drowned Man
  Sydney Lea (1980)

With Akhmatova at the
  Black Gates
  Stephen Berg (1981)

Dream Flights
  Dave Smith (1981)

More Trouble with the
  Obvious
  Michael Van Walleghen (1981)

The American Book of
  the Dead
  Jim Barnes (1982)

The Floating Candles
  Sydney Lea (1982)

Northbook
  Frederick Morgan (1982)

Collected Poems, 1930-83
  Josephine Miles (1983)

The River Painter
  Emily Grosholz (1984)

Healing Song for the
  Inner Ear
  Michael S. Harper (1984)

The Passion of the Right-
  Angled Man
  T. R. Hummer (1984)

Dear John, Dear Coltrane
  Michael S. Harper (1985)

Poems from the Sangamon
  John Knoepfle (1985)

In It
  Stephen Berg (1986)

The Ghosts of Who We Were
  Phyllis Thompson (1986)

Moon in a Mason Jar
  Robert Wrigley (1986)

Lower-Class Heresy
  T. R. Hummer (1987)

Poems: New and Selected
  Frederick Morgan (1987)

Furnace Harbor: A Rhapsody
  of the North Country
  Philip D. Church (1988)

Bad Girl, with Hawk
  Nance Van Winckel (1988)

Blue Tango
  Michael Van Walleghen (1989)

Eden
  Dennis Schmitz (1989)

Waiting for Poppa at the
  Smithtown Diner
  Peter Serchuk (1990)

Great Blue
  Brendan Galvin (1990)

What My Father Believed
  Robert Wrigley (1991)

Something Grazes Our Hair
  S. J. Marks (1991)

Walking the Blind Dog
  G. E. Murray (1992)

The Sawdust War
  Jim Barnes (1992)

The God of Indeterminacy
  Sandra McPherson (1993)

Off-Season at the Edge of
  the World
  Debora Greger (1994)

Counting the Black Angels
  Len Roberts (1994)

National Poetry Series

Eroding Witness
  Nathaniel Mackey (1985)
Selected by Michael Harper

Palladium
  Alice Fulton (1986)
Selected by Mark Strand

Cities in Motion
  Sylvia Moss (1987)
Selected by Derek Walcott

The Hand of God and a Few
  Bright Flowers
  William Olsen (1988)
Selected by David Wagoner

The Great Bird of Love
  Paul Zimmer (1989)
Selected by William Stafford

Stubborn
  Roland Flint (1990)
Selected by Dave Smith

The Surface
  Laura Mullen (1991)
Selected by C. K. Williams

The Dig
  Lynn Emanuel (1992)
Selected by Gerald Stern

My Alexandria
  Mark Doty (1993)
Selected by Philip Levine

The High Road to Taos
  Martin Edmunds (1994)
Selected by Donald Hall

Other Poetry Volumes

Her Soul beneath the Bone:
  Women's Poetry on Breast Cancer
  Edited by Leatrice Lifshitz (1988)

Days from a Dream Almanac
Dennis Tedlock (1990)

Working Classics: Poems on
   Industrial Life
   Edited by Peter Oresick and
   Nicholas Coles (1990)

Hummers, Knucklers, and Slow Curves:
   Contemporary Baseball Poems
   Edited by Don Johnson (1991)

The Double Reckoning of Christopher
   Columbus
   Barbara Helfgott Hyett (1992)

Selected Poems
   Jean Garrigue (1992)

New and Selected Poems, 1962-92
   Laurence Lieberman (1993)